Amanda Jane's Fun Shoes

Amanda Jane's Fun Shoes

✦

and Other Paternal Epiphanies

Dr. Rob Holdsambeck
Clinical Psychologist/ Board
Certified Behavior Analyst
Instructor of Human Sexuality,
Allan Hancock College

iUniverse, Inc.
New York Lincoln Shanghai

Amanda Jane's Fun Shoes
and Other Paternal Epiphanies

iUniverse books may be ordered through booksellers or by contacting:

iUniverse
2021 Pine Lake Road, Suite 100
Lincoln, NE 68512
www.iuniverse.com
1-800-Authors (1-800-288-4677)

ISBN-13: 978-0-595-38120-3 (pbk)
ISBN-13: 978-0-595-82488-5 (ebk)
ISBN-10: 0-595-38120-0 (pbk)
ISBN-10: 0-595-82488-9 (ebk)

Printed in the United States of America

Contents

Introduction

I've spent the better part of my adult life trying to understand people and what makes us see things so differently. Along the way, I've accumulated some great experiences that have helped. I managed to get my doctorate in psychology, finish my postdoctoral internship, get licensed as psychologist, attain my board certification as a behavior analyst, and even get the elusive tenured position at a local college teaching, among other courses, human sexuality. Even with all my professional experience, I have always learned the most from those who share my daily life. As luck would have it, I became the father of daughters. To be more precise, I have a wife and three charming daughters.

As these ladies will attest, we do see the world differently at times. It is very possible that being a man among so many women sets the stage for some of those differences. I grew up with brothers (and an older sister). I played sports all through my schooling on all male squads. I enlisted in the service at a time when the military academies, flight schools, and most of my own basic training were, if not fully restricted to men, segregated by gender. I really enjoyed the company of women, but there was some validity to the claim that my "feminine side" was poorly developed.

Webster's College Dictionary defines an epiphany as "a sudden, intuitive perception of or insight into reality or the essential meaning of something, often initiated by some simple, commonplace occurrence" (Costello,1991, p.450). The title of this book, *Amanda Jane's Fun Shoes and Other Paternal Epiphanies*, came from a series of conversations and encounters between me and my daughters and several other significant women in my life. Sometimes these insights were revealed after many years of experience and multiple encounters. Other times, however, they were triggered by something as simple as a comment made in passing. In the case of this book, it was a comment made about a pair of shoes.

One day after work, I listened as Amanda Jane ("daughter third and last" as she is known to me) and her older sister were discussing their latest "fun shoes". For some time after that, I tried to understand why I found that particular phrase so interesting. I consulted my friends, my students, and even several professional colleagues. I found that for many people, the idea that shoes can be "fun" makes perfect sense. Some others, mostly the dads in my group, had heard the phrase but had never really given it much thought. In fact, most of the dads with whom I consulted spoke of their footwear by its color or by its function (hiking boots, running shoes, work shoes, etc). This probably seems a like a trivial difference to some. However, if you possess this "limited functional view" of footwear (that is how my daughter describes my own perspective), you probably also possess a small number of shoes. It is also quite logical that if shoes can make statements and convey attitudes, one needs many, many pairs to express the full range of things that need expressing. Recognizing differences in the way people perceive ordinary things does not imply that one worldview or the other is more accurate. It does, however, help this dad understand the challenges inherent in gender differences.

Picking Nits with Einstein

On my wall at work hangs a poster of Albert Einstein. My favorite quote of his is written on the poster, and it goes like this: "I want to know God's thoughts, the rest are details." I really like people who understand things in a profound way, especially when they can boil that understanding down into what appears to be a simple, parsimonious formula. The complex relationships between energy, mass, and the relative speed of light are things that most of us do not ponder frequently. All we seem to know is that we don't have enough time, and we are running out of spaces to put things. It is also a subject that is way too deep for me to think about very long without feeling really stupid or getting a headache. However, for whatever reason, this gifted man spent a lot of time and effort on that problem, and his equations became legendary.

If you can find the time and the place, you should watch apes or monkeys go about their days. The females often engage in a type of grooming and nurturing behavior that involves picking lice and nits off the coats of their kin. It seems to be a regular and somewhat pleasant process for both the picker and the pickee. I am sure there is someone focused on the tragedy that befalls the tiny nits, but that would not be me. For reasons that I do not understand, the term "nitpicking," over time, has come to take on a very different connotation than what the monkeys convey. To be called a "nitpicker" does not mean that you are literally picking nits. It means that you are not focused on the things that seem important to the person you are criticizing. In fact, the pickee may feel that the picker is incessantly pointing out small annoyances, and somehow is not capable of seeing the big picture.

Over time, I have learned a few things about negotiating business and consulting contracts. In a contract, lawyers put in all sorts of details. In fact, contracts are full of them. If someone does not pay careful attention to those details, bad things happen. Now, you may decide to outsource the creation or monitoring of those details, but the less you know, the more chances you take that something will fall apart. I would imagine that the same principal applies to most aspects of life.

My dad was an engineer, a pilot, and a graduate of Auburn, Princeton and MIT, and he could pick nits. Most engineers are pretty good detail folks. My dad admired Einstein even more than I do but for a totally different reason. My dad had an engineer's understanding of math, so he could understand the relationship between space and time mathematically. I, however, admire Einstein for his passion to understand the universe, his willingness to apply the gifts he was given, and the sheer volume of the great thoughts that poured out from his work. I am pretty sure it frustrated the heck out of Dad that I was not willing to properly do the work involved to understand how beautiful math really is. I know it frustrated me that he didn't want me to skip the math and take Einstein at his word. We were on opposite sides of the nitpicking equation.

My poster of Einstein also shows something else: the man did not seem to be overly concerned with how his hair looked. It was perhaps a detail about the universe that just didn't concern him. It has a certain casual flair to it that I find appealing. Of course, at this point in my life, the idea of hair growing wildly out of the top of my head is appealing because mine isn't. Relatively speaking, Einstein's hair looks pretty darn good to me.

Another fact about Einstein that people often overlook is that in 1895, he was denied admission to his college of choice in Zurich. It seems that someone had issues with his essays. This little diversion sent him off to seek other work at a patent office. I have not seen the graded admissions test, but my guess is that someone was picking nits with this very great mind. Einstein had a way of posing issues that was very profound, but that could also fly in the face of logic. (Try conceptualizing light as both a wave and a particle some time.) It could be that the admissions reader was just more concerned with nits and less concerned with the universe. Either way, it didn't deter Einstein from eventually making his points. Some people have argued that his time away from the university allowed him the space to develop some pretty contrary notions that might not have been developed if he had been subjected too early to academic nit-picking.

It may seem odd to some, but you don't have to be overly smart to get a doctorate in something. You have to be smart to get through high school and just wise enough or lucky enough to get through college. Most of the rest of the skills you need involve persistence, support, and learning to attend to the details of graduate school that are the most relevant to getting your degree. Fortunately for me, persistence is probably the most important of those listed attributes, and not attending to details.

Like many professionals, I was persistent enough in higher education to have earned the right to put a bunch of initials after my name. Despite that, I have been reminded at times that I am not especially good at picking up on important details that cross my daily life. When those reminders hit me in the wrong way or hit me too often, I feel as though I am being nitpicked. And, all things being relative, I may just be right. The trouble is that being right about something does not necessarily help in certain situations. Relationships are complex formulas. As it turns out, nitpicking and attending to details are best viewed as relative terms.

Take my first daughter Kirsten's wedding. Now, that is an important time in the life of a daughter and the life of a father. I prepared for that time of life. I knew it would come, and I saved up some money. Kirsten had not chosen an easy course earlier in life, but she was clearly on the right road now, and I actually like the man she had chosen. I knew that there might be personal things I needed to work on, like playing well with others, so I tried to be more pleasant than usual on the wedding day.

Funny thing about events like weddings: they don't always follow a precise formula, or so my theory goes. Another theory has it that they do follow a precise formula, and I was just doing all the calculations poorly. The event involved details that boggle my mind to this day. My role, however, became clear from the wedding group's first meeting. Our particular wedding group consisted of my daughter, my wife, the event coordinator, the mother of the groom and me. In case you have not planned a wedding yet, let me clarify the role of Father of the Bride.

The group asked me for my opinion on a variety of things. To begin with, there was food. I love food, so they asked, and I opened with the notion that everyone loves the way I cook my ribs, so why not just serve ribs? That idea was dismissed at approximately the speed of light added to the amount of time it took each woman in the room to turn her head in my direction and scowl. The next thing I was asked had something to do with planning the site of the reception. Now, I have a pretty nice house. I even have a perfectly good jukebox, so I offered the notion of doing it at home. Again, the slow turns and cold glances notified me that I was really not getting the process at all.

I am happy report that I did learn a lot from this nit-picking exercise of wedding planning. Nits are important details, and it is really nice when someone takes on the smaller tasks so that you can focus on the truly important role that you are expected to play in the event. As a father of the bride, the mantra goes something like this: "Open checkbook, close mouth; open checkbook, close mouth, breathe in, and breathe out as you become the willing financier." As potentially challenging as that mantra sounds, it actually came to pass in just that way. Whenever I get down about the confronting the inevitable conflicts of daily life, I remember my poster of Einstein. His comment about wanting to know God's thoughts and how the rest are just details, helps to restore my smile.

Primordial Ooze

Scientists often refer to the base elements from which life took its original form as primordial ooze or soup. I always picture the ooze as a hot cauldron of elements gurgling, smoking, and generally mixing things up. I'm not sure that it has ever been proved, but it is an interesting concept that always reminds me of how we are all built of the same stuff. However, that is not to say that we end up the same just because we share the same chemical elements. For example, due to the odd workings of the Y chromosome, some fetuses develop a male set of organs, and those that don't get the Y influence continue to develop into females.

As a husband and the father of three daughters, I am acutely aware of how the strange monthly ebb and flow of hormones can make daily events change their meanings. Movies that are sad become tragic. A person's annoying eating habits are suddenly disgusting. Some women share their feelings overtly, and others are more subtle. However, disgust is not really so easy to hide, even if you are not talking. Just as suddenly as they changed the first time, the meanings of those same events change again. Tragic movies go back to being sad, and sloppy eating is once again a tolerable annoyance.

Dads who miss the signs of impending changes in the balance of hormones stirring in the ooze are often blindsided. Dads who know the signs are still often blindsided, but in the interest of education, let's discuss a few of these signals. Often, my girls' eating behavior begins to shift in the direction of sweets and chocolate. Sometimes I observed this change directly. Other times, I just noticed that small candy wrappers would be piled up in the trash or in some corner of a room. I quickly learned that during that phase, my girls were just not that comfortable sharing their chocolate with me or even answering questions about their chocolate or, God forbid, being teased about how the chocolate might be related to something hormonal that was happening.

The next stage, although outwardly perceptible, was really difficult to pick up on, but let me try to describe it. The way they look at me changes: one smiles less and shakes her head more, another one's clothes don't fit right. She makes a few comments about "feeling heavy," and then in a short while, the changes in mood get dramatically worse. It becomes evident that I am doing or have done something disgusting or hurtful. Exactly what I did is not exactly the issue. I suspect that other fathers of daughters have had that experience.

During this second phase, if I am around, whatever goes wrong is going to be my fault. If I am fortunate enough to be away, this hormonal crankiness might get projected onto someone else, but it is still probably linked to you in some fashion. Oh, and in case you are wondering what it is like to live with many women, there is this wonderfully perplexing phenomenon called menstrual synchronicity. When it works well, the women in my house cry together at the commercials, cry at the movies, complain to each other, hug, and make up with each other, and so on. Crying over commercials is an extreme example, but I have witnessed this behavior myself. If I ever attempt to intrude upon this female bonding process—say, to add a male perspective or, worse yet, to suggest that the house feels a bit like a set from *The Exorcist*—I have to be prepared for heads to turn and vile things to occur. I do travel out of town on business at least one time each month, but there is no truth to the rumor that I schedule business meetings for the first week after the chocolate candy wrappers start piling up.

If you live with women, as I do, you get to join in this journey whether it happens to fit into your schedule or not. I am here to provide witness to another sad fact: when the ooze is churning and bubbling and such, it is not a conscious process; it just happens. It can catch men and women alike by surprise despite the fact that it occurs over and over and over. And if that were not enough, the women in your life will probably tell you that their behavior is not related to their hormones and you do not understand, and you never will.

As if this cycle were not enough to deal with, there is another part of the story. Women are not born menstruating, and most who live long enough will not die menstruating. This means that their bodies have to adjust to starting and stopping this odd hormonal roulette. Starting early can be an issue. Starting late can be an issue. Adjusting to irregularities can be an issue. And most importantly, adjusting to stopping can be a huge issue. In case you are not aware, it is not uncommon for that last stage to take a decade!

They Smell Babies

While it is certainly not true of all women, my women love babies. In fact, some psychological studies actually show that one of the most powerful and potent scents that arouse women's senses is none other than baby powder. My family is expecting a second grandbaby soon, and I have had several occasions to observe a gathering of women when a new baby is around and another is expected. It is their gender's equivalent of a man coming into a group of buddies with a brand-new boat. They stare at it, ask all about where it has been, and dream about where it will go. They reminisce about their own experiences and generally gush. But even that metaphor does not fully capture the experience of my women's behavior around babies.

My sister called soon after the birth of my grandson. After some brief chitchat on weight and length and such, she actually asked me, "How does he smell?" That is not a question that most of my gender would ever think to ask, much less to actually ask. Usually, most of us are very pleased not to smell anything coming from the baby. All smelling is not the same. My women will pick up a baby, bring it to their noses, and inhale like the room was running out of air. Slowly, a smile breaks over their faces, and an expression follows that approximates bliss. I love my kids, but I can honestly say that I have never had that same olfactory experience with babies. A new boat or a new sports car though, now that is a smell worth inhaling.

The adoration of babies is not necessarily a bad thing. In fact, having folks who are attracted to babies is necessary for our survival as a species. But there is a problem lurking here, as well. Babies and children and, heaven knows, teenagers, take an extraordinary amount of work. Call it love, call it parenting, call it whatever, but it takes a ton of time. I've spent some time as a single dad and a lot of time working with moms. Trust me: one of the most common things I hear is that they are tired. You could be tempted to try to fix that for them or analyze it with them, but you will fail. They love their children, they worry about them, and they are exhausted by them.

There is another issue here. Some women have children, either by plan or by lack of planning, and some women do not, either by choice, by circumstance, or even as a result of fertility issues. I know several women who do not have children that are consistently confronted by others to explain why they have made that choice. This has got to be infuriating over time. If you choose not to do something as exhausting and perilous as rearing kids, why should you have to explain yourself? It is the classic double standard. My friend Julie, who does not have children, put it about as succinctly as I have heard it put: "I just don't feel the need to breed." Sounds to me like people should take her at her word.

Believe it or not, not all men are into fishing, sailing, or water-skiing. Most of us, however, are still interested in boats. We are just happy to let other men own them and care for them. Even those who are not at all interested in heading out into the open water are seldom asked to explain what is missing in their psyche that causes them to not feel the need to fish. It is also true, however, that some men buy the darn boat and go through a lot of trouble, only to realize that they did not want a boat in the first place. It sounded like a good idea, it looked sexy in the magazine, but now it just takes up space in the garage. I realize the analogy is a bit weak, but when they are new, or at least properly cleaned up, a good boat smells sweet.

Trouble in Paradise

Psychologists have known for a long time that stories do not have to be taken literally to have powerful effects. This first one may not be the oldest, but it might just be the most powerful story of all. If you are a product of a culture influenced by Christianity, Judaism, or Islam, you probably know very well how this story goes. God created man and left him to roam in paradise, but alas, paradise was not complete. Perhaps food was just too easy to get, or maybe it was that football and big screen TVs had yet to make the scene. But whatever the reason, man felt alone, and woman was created. In most biblical translations she is called Eve. After God created this first woman, everything was perfect until that ugly incident with the forbidden fruit. The first people were given everything, with only one thing explicitly listed as off-limits. Things went well for a brief time, but eventually a third character appears in the form of a serpent.

There are many versions of what happens next, but most center on the notion that the serpent gets Eve to see the benefits of eating from the tree of knowledge. The promise of knowledge, freedom, and the exercise of free will lead to the seduction of Eve and eventually of Adam, as well. Soon after that, they get caught eating the wrong fruit and get busted for being aware of their nakedness, and lose paradise forever. To drive home the point, God punishes the three characters very severely. The snake is doomed to crawl and forever be stepped on by people. The woman is sentenced to pain and suffering in childbirth, and worse yet, she is condemned to be subservient to her husband. Adam, for his part, is tossed out of the garden and sentenced to work the soil for the foreseeable future. According to some biblical scholars, that was about eight hundred years of hard labor. The message does not appear to be overly subtle: the evil temptress questing for knowledge has spoiled things for a long time to come—as in, forever.

Now, you can and probably should argue that this chain of events was the serpent's fault, but that misses the point entirely. God in this story clearly holds all three players responsible for their transgressions. At issue is not whether women are to blame, but rather that they often do get blamed and sometimes feel guilty regardless of their actual guilt or innocence. The issue here is not whether we should blame women when things go awry but only that history teaches us that women can be tempting targets. My youngest daughter will feel guilty and will even apologize after knocking an opponent down in a soccer match. That is not exactly the reaction I felt after a particularly solid tackle when I was her age.

Another thing this story implies is that a real woman can get men to do anything. In psychological studies, women have been asked to order their fantasies from the most intriguing to the least appealing. Being thought of as irresistible is at the top of many women's lists. It is an intriguing thought. After all, if Eve got Adam to disobey God by offering him fruit while standing around naked, what chance do men have today? This ancient concept of woman as the irresistible evil temptress is still with us today. If you want to read any of these studies you can consult the ninth edition of the classic text on Human Sexuality "*Our Sexuality*" by Crooks and Baur (Thompson Wadsworth, 2005).

Fun Shoes and Practical Cars

I must admit that the idea that a pair of shoes can be fun does not come naturally to me. I have always thought that shoes are either comfortable or not. To most members of my gender, they are something we grow accustomed to, and we are generally bummed when they give out. For whatever the reason, the women in my family acquired different ideas. Shoes make statements. Shoes have attitudes. They can even be "fun." When they choose shoes, the fact that they may or may not be really comfortable is, to some, further down the decision-making tree. I have worn shoes that didn't feel right, and it was not fun. I tossed them as soon as I could.

I think I grasp the concept of fashion statements. On occasion, I even wear a necktie. I just think that sometimes the statements are wrong. I am coming to think that there is some sort of plot against women in this department. Many of the women I see seem to choose fashionable clothes with little regard to what their bodies look like, and even less regard to what their body parts are supposed to do. This is not always the case. Indeed, there are some fine examples of women making functional, attractive fashion statements out there that often lead other women to feel guilty for not measuring up. But by and large, most women don't seem particularly pleased with the way their clothes fit, or the way their clothes make them look, or the particular direction of the latest fashion. However, they do feel a tremendous pressure to look a particular way. I think that is why some women like to buy new stuff—a lot!

I went to the shoe store the other day because my black pair had worn out, and my mother-in-law noticed them in church and commented, "As a professional, you could probably afford to get a new pair." I discovered that men like me classify shoes by function (work boots, running shoes, church shoes, etc.). In most cases, once a particular style is found to function the right way, the style is in for the foreseeable future. The possible exception lies in the preponderance of younger guys lusting over this or that athletic shoe. But even then, I think the key to their choice is their belief that somehow athletic shoes will make them run faster or jump higher or rap or something, rather than make a statement. Until I overheard two of my daughters describing some totally "fun shoes," I really had never thought to attach such adjectives to footwear. On television and in the stores, men's shoes are described as cool, functional, fashionable, or comfortable, but never as fun.

Now, the flip side to making statements with shoes is driving practical cars and paying absolutely no attention to their rims. My goddaughters, Jacqueline and Kelly, are new to the driving arena. One drives a truck, and one is lusting after one of those pint-sized, super cool Mini Coopers. Those two vehicles make statements. I am pretty sure the truck was not picked because it could haul large amounts of garbage to the dump. I am also sure that the other's Mini Cooper may never materialize because of her parents' practicality.

My point, however, is larger. Although my women started their driving years with the correct notion that what you drive does, indeed, make a statement, at some point most people would rather have a vehicle that "just works for them." In my family system, that seems to have coincided with the arrival of children. When I met my wife, she drove a red sports car. Prior to that, she owned a perfectly useless, but sexy, British made sports car. Add kids to the mix and presto, the beige minivan and all that it signifies suddenly became her vehicle of choice.

Getting young children into and out of car seats can be an ordeal for newly initiated parents. As children get a little older, they have friends and teammates who need hauling, and most of them, it seems, are hungry and come with snacks. My girls also had a lot of stuff that apparently was essential to travel that needed a place in the vehicle to be set down while they were attending to other stuff. I have actually overheard women describe their vehicle with the phrase "it just works for me," and I panicked that they were also describing men at some level. I have had many in-depth conversations with women over the years, and not one that I can recall with a woman beyond young-adulthood involved how good chrome rims make a car look better.

Now, if a person believes that shoes make statements, then she will need many, many pairs. After all, there is much to be said. If a person believes that shoes are for a specific purpose, then he will feel no compulsion to change them out if, perhaps, the styles change over the decades. If, however, a person feels that a vehicle needs to make a statement, then that person may need different statements at different times of his life. My life to date may be a good example.

My first car was a beat-up, barely-running Mustang convertible. The first item I repaired on it was the eight-track stereo. That car made the very cool statement that I was as free as the wind, into rock music, and generally unconcerned about safety. As time passed, I converted a van, and it even had a bed. That was, I thought, a rather succinct statement that my military service was over, I was free from the burdens of haircuts and uniforms, and I was headed for California. One time, I bought a truck, and I immediately went for the upgraded rims. Keep in mind that no one would ever think to describe me as a handyman, and I am certainly not the guy going back and forth to the hardware store to get more lumber. I eventually gave the truck to my daughter back when her vehicle selections were not influenced in the least by thoughts of hauling children. After the truck, I even had a convertible sports car in my middle age, until I realized that getting in and out was too big a hassle for the statement I was making.

At each stage, I would bring these vehicles home proudly and display my latest automotive statement. Instead of affirming or even sharing my admiration, my wife would ask bunch of silly questions. Questions like, "Wasn't the old one still working?" Or, "Do we really need a sports car at this point in our lives?" My wife and her friends all drive cars that "work for them": beige minivans, SUVs with abundant cup holders, and the like. They speak of ones that haul kids, kids' friends, and stuff from church. They drive cars whose seats fold up or down easily. They keep cars that are large enough for everyone to fit into together for long trips, as if that were ever a good plan! They may have started driving with statement cars in mind, or they may not have. But clearly at this stage, their cars just have to "work for them." They may secretly lust over sports cars with great rims, but I doubt it.

In my field of psychology, there is a tendency to go deep when issues come up. Misunderstandings between women and men have deep roots, and one should pay those of us in the profession dearly for insight. However, I wish to offer up one simple thought that may speak to some: If you find yourself bemused by a loved one who does not fully appreciate how a great set of rims makes a statement about the car owner, consider the last time you felt the urge to squeeze your feet into a pair of fun shoes. For a dad like me, that answer would be never.

Graduating Magna Comb Loudly

At one time or another in my life, I have always had an issue with hair. When I was a boy, I had what was known as a cowlick, a clump of hair that stuck up in front as if a cow had just licked my face. I used to lick my hand and try to make it go another way, but it generally popped back up. One time in middle school, my dad put a bowl over my head and cut my hair really close, and it looked like—well, it looked like my dad had put a bowl over my head and then proceeded with the haircut anyway. Eventually, I went to college on an Air Force scholarship that required that I cut my hair very short during a time when it was cool to have long hair. I am now at the awkward stage that some men face where we lose it rapidly, and quite frankly, we just run out of good choices. But I really had no sense of the importance of hair, nor of the care and feeding of hair, nor of the statements hair can make, until I started listening to women.

My two eldest daughters Kirsten and Kassandra have great thick hair that they obviously did not inherit from their dad. When they were staying with me when they were young, I had the task of getting them ready for school, which involves a bit of planning, to say the least. I was pretty good at most aspects of the deal but never really got the hair thing. I know this because one of my daughters told me that her teacher could always tell when she was living with her dad because of her hair. Ouch.

I did try. I bought special products to wash, shine, and condition. I bought tools that looked like they could be helpful in the process, but I never made it past the directions. I tried this braid or that clip, and it would never go right. I consulted my male friends, and they were clueless. I just figured that I needed to learn some more about how women solve problems when they are stumped, so I asked a woman. My friend Cathy told me that women "network." In other words, they seek out people who may at some point in the future be of help to them and make reciprocal relationships. It sounded like a really good idea.

My first networking opportunity occurred in the health club I went to most mornings. I actually taught a college course in racquetball there in the early hours, before my other job started. So I would take my two little ones—nicely dressed, I might add—with combs, brushes, and assorted things with me. I went to work looking helpless, dazed, and confused, and bingo! A nice lady who knew me and worked in the front office asked me about my "problem." I told her that I just didn't get hair. She scooped up my girls and told them not to worry, that she loved hair and would love it if they would stop by in the morning and allow her to work her magic. And she did, and they loved it. Networks are a very cool thing.

There is a darker side to this issue, however. Hair is beautiful, but beautiful hair is not easy. Worse yet, getting beautiful hair is complex and, at times, quite ugly. Some women have this fantasy fueled by the media that it shouldn't be that way. Just wash in this or that, and poof, perfect hair! But it is just a fantasy. Hair needs to be cleaned, conditioned, colored, curled, and brushed, all on a fairly regular schedule. My goddaughter, with curly hair, brushes hers out to be straight. My third daughter, with straight hair, has started curling it. Women, it seems, have a lot to do in this department, and it's not too great a stretch to imply that they are not always thrilled with the process, or with the results. Bad hair is simply awful. Some women will avoid perfectly good meals when they are really hungry in some kind of weird protest of their uncooperative hair. Good hair is not good enough. It needs checking, pushing around, and squeezing or poofing, or something else. Worse yet, great hair doesn't stay great and is at the mercy of things that are darn hard to control, like wind and fog and humidity. At times, women need to sleep, and that is not something that treats anyone's hair kindly. A direct consequence of the aforementioned difficulties is that they spend time, money, and a lot of emotional energy in an area where something more could always be done.

The ladies in my life are nice people. They generally do not cuss openly, and they seldom voice homicidal intentions, at least in my presence. However, you don't have to be living with them long to know they have hair tantrums. Brushes fly. Muddled cursing of this or that styling device can be heard before they even leave the house. "I hate my bangs!" "I can't get it to do anything right!" "My hair is just stupid!" And it only gets worse when they run a little behind schedule. These women can have a bona fide temper tantrum before the day even gets formally started.

I have learned over time that I really play no role in this morning dance. It is best if I steer clear of it all together. And I do try. Sometimes I forget that lesson, and the results are never pretty. I once pointed out to my wife that her cursing about her difficulties with her abundant hair was like me cursing about my pants getting too loose around the middle or cursing that I pay too much in taxes because I made too much money. That particular discussion, while technically brilliant, was ill timed and exploded on takeoff. I guess it's not fair to say I play no role. My job, it seems, is to always notice when one of them changes the style and to always comment that it makes her look good. To be honest, I seldom get this one right.

If you really want to make a woman happy, tell her your fantasy is to wash her hair. (It probably goes without saying here, but I am not advising this as a pick-up line. This one is reserved for those you know very well.) Washing and conditioning her hair is a role she will let you play. However, you are best advised to ask her how she likes it done first, because even though it sounds like everyone should do it one way, they don't. And the directions on the bottles are of no help; if you follow them correctly, you will be rinsing and repeating so long that she will leave you.

Let me make one final comment on hair. I heard once that a woman thinks about her hair as often as a man does about sex. I'm not at all sure how the researchers collected that data. All I can say for sure is that the women I know think about their hair a lot more than the men I know think about sex. It's not that men don't think about sex a lot; it's just that if we think about it that hard and work at it that much and have issues with it that constantly, we would probably get arrested or at least sent to therapy.

Heifers

It's not that I don't have guy friends; I do. I golf with men. I join in this odd ritual called fantasy football with men. I have good male friends, and they mean a lot to me. These are just different than my friendships with women. My guy friends and I play things together. I have never had the desire to gather as a tribe, beat drums, and do bonding experiences. I've heard that some men do, but it is just not in my nature. OK, to be honest, I did once do something like that. It was called Indian Guides and was designed to let dads have a better relationship with their kids. The whole drum-beating and chanting thing was not about us bonding with each other. Chief Pinot Noir (we were, after all, a California tribe), was merely trying to cultivate our children's appreciation of Native American rhythms, as well as their fathers' appreciation of the appropriate modern libation. I am happy to report that even without the presence of adult females, we never lost a camper, at least not for long.

I do often play golf in a foursome of men, and I think that is about the right number for proper mixing. If one or another member of the foursome starts to become a pain, we simply form another group. Sometimes a member might get busy and drop out, and we will add another. Sometimes we play with only two or three, and it still works. After all, we are not there to bond; we are playing. If you watched us closely, you might not think it was fun playing given the foul language and the occasional club tossing. However, I can assure you that even though the schedule of reinforcement might be lean, it is, in fact, fun.

The women I know are different: women bond. They form bonds and take great strides to keep those bonds intact, even when things get rocky. Bonding starts early and, I believe, goes in cycles throughout life. One peak surrounds the teen years and early adulthood. My daughters all have had strong bonds with friends. I have not always been the most accepting of those they chose to bond with, but it is my belief that people often make poor choices and that part of my role is to help them see that. You can guess right away that this created a certain degree of tension at times between my brood and me. I have lived with it, and I know it to be true that women's early friendship bonds are very, very, very important to them. They cause each other joy, pain, and a whole host of emotions in between, but they are strongly bonded nonetheless.

Men and women often write journals to me, as a part of the class I teach. In fact I require that my students write down their opinions about the material we discuss each day in class. Some young ladies occasionally make this kind of statement: "I don't really have any female friends. I think I just like men better." At first, I was naïve enough to take that as a compliment to my own gender. (In reality, it doesn't take much for me to go down that road.) The problem, though, is deeper than that. In the best of worlds, women bond well with other women. That is not to say that some girls don't prefer to play with boys as they are developing. Some do. However, as they transition into adulthood, some men will adopt female friends and require very little reciprocity from them. The men are at first curious about the women, sometimes flattered to be around them, and very often interested in developing a structure that will include "benefits." Women sometimes mistake all that attention and think that guys just treat them better. Then they do something silly like settle into a romantic relationship with one, and all heck breaks loose because the relationship suddenly keeps getting sidelined into discussions of what we in the field call perceived reciprocity. That simply means that it is important in a relationship for both sides to feel that they are getting a fair share. Gradually a man and a woman in a relationship may come to feel like they aren't getting as much from their partner as they think they should be getting. It can start with a missed date, a late arrival, an awkward sexual exchange, or even something like who listened to whose problems longer. It matters very little whether what happened is actually fair; all that matters is that both parties see it as fair. This is so important because perceived reciprocity is actually one of the better predictors of how long a romantic relationship will actually last. However, this book is not really about how all men and all women relate to each other but more about how the women I know relate to each other. Namely, how they network.

You see networks everywhere. Walk a trail in the woods, and you may just encounter wildlife, but you will probably see groups of women walking. Go out to lunch, and you will not only see groups huddling around food and eating but also, more importantly, talking. They sometimes shop in groups, meet for coffee, and nowadays, link together on the Internet through e-mail, personal spaces, and instant messages. Daughter third and last can be on the computer with multiple friends and still maintain a decent phone conversation with those same friends and others.

Sometimes they develop odd habits like shopping for a whole week every year. Some even develop names for their groups of friends, like "the shopping group," or "the Jazzercise group," or MOPS (which seems to be a church-inspired way of helping moms deal with preschoolers), or CWA (which, by the way, I learned stood for Chicks With Attitudes). Far and away the weirdest name I ever heard for such a group of women came from my sister-in-law, Colleen.

Colleen was reared on a farm outside of Little Rock, Arkansas. She recently met a nice man and moved to a small town in Texas named Bryan. She is an attractive, smart woman. But she and her friends back home actually refer to themselves as "Badass Heifers"! And they mean it with affection. If you have ever spent time observing cows, and you got into it too deeply, you are probably a farmer, a rancher, a vet, or just somebody with way too much time on your hands. I am none of the above. I do teach, however, and have spent time on a farm and even milked a cow once, although not very well. I can tell you that I have never thought of that beast as a favorable model. Truth be known, when I do think of them favorably, it is as a nice vehicle for dairy products or a very tasty sirloin. If you stare into the eyes of a cow, you get very little back. They chew all the time, and they emit obnoxious smells and byproducts all around. My sense is that they are not thinking of much other than whatever just happened to pop up from one of their many stomachs and when they need to refill that stomach. I tease my students at times that they give me that same "bovine stare" when they are spacing out in class. But unflattering as it may be, those gals from Little Rock got a hoot out of that name, and it stuck.

I came home from golfing with a friend I have known since high school. We lead different lives, but I like him. He and I joke a lot, but he gets mad at his own game. So being men, the rest of the foursome and I make fun of him, and, being a man, he gives it back, and that is as far as the conversation goes. His wife is wonderful, and he has great and challenging children. My point is this: the first question my wife asked upon returning from a game of golf with him was, "So how are his wife and kids?" I didn't have the time or the good sense to make something up, so I just said, "I don't know." That produced a wicked look that I'm pretty sure was one part "You're joking, right?" and one part "That is so insensitive to your friend."

Being the sensitive guy that I am, I was really hurt by that. So I thought it was a good thing to point out to her that men sometimes like to just play games without talking about families. And with men, personal questions are not play; they are hard work. And playing is bonding in some ways. And he knows that I would do anything for him and his family without my having to question him on the golf course about personal stuff. And…Actually, she left before any of that got out.

Ca-Ching, Bling-Bling

Money is one of those powerful things in modern life that permeates the structures between and among men and women, and especially dads and daughters. Some families do not discuss it at all, but some others fight over it with some regularity. Often, family members have issues with power, the distribution of resources, who does what for whom, and a whole host of other things related to money. This may be a byproduct of our culture. I've not personally done any research on the topic, but the concept of freedom from things (rather than freedom to do or have things) strikes a chord with me. In fact, some people are just in denial about money altogether, and that is why I've gathered my thoughts on the topic.

I have heard some people say they are not concerned with money. Sometimes they say this after a prolonged fight about issues related to money. Sometimes people say this because they don't understand money and don't want to focus on it. Life is rich, and life is busy, and we can only focus on so much. In the event that I am wrong, if you are one of those truly unconcerned, I invite you to send me yours (or at least any you have left over). I will happily find a use for it. I won't even charge you a dime. Send it any way you like, but please don't delay, as I may not be able to take everyone's leftover money forever. I will add this caveat, because I really want you to send me money: if you don't pay attention to your money for long enough, someone else will come along and just take it. If you bury it in the backyard, it may stick around, but it won't be worth nearly as much as you think. And besides, that would deprive you of the pleasure of mailing it to me. And I do want you to have that pleasure.

In psychological terms, money is described as a "conditioned generalized reinforcer." At least it was at my school. Let me explain that phrase and how it relates to our approach towards money. A reinforcer is a consequence that strengthens behavior. Primary reinforcers do that without any learning or conditioning (think of food and water and sex). They are very powerful but somewhat contingent upon a certain state of deprivation (think of water when you are not thirsty).

A conditioned reinforcer is one with which we have to have experiences in order for it to be effective in shaping our behavior. In other words, we learn to associate it with primary reinforcers, either directly or indirectly. An example of that might be if approval is paired with nurturing: we might do things for approval, and "approval" becomes a whole class of rewards, as well. Now, imagine if there were reinforcers out there that were learned and general. In other words, they can apply to lots of states of deprivation, lots of states of approval, and can even be stored up for later use. That is where the concept of money belongs. Not everyone you meet understands that. Some people think money is just something that is given to you. Many think of it as something other people get that they don't. Members of this last group just don't like the idea that there might be a relationship between money and behavior.

While the power of money is based on faith (your faith that it will be worth something), money isn't, by itself, good or evil. It just is. People can do good things with money (like sending it to me), or they can do evil things with money (say, funding terrorists). They can do good things to get money (such as helping kids learn to read), or they can do evil things to get money (stealing might fit here). There is actually a continuum that stretches all the way from good to evil that sometimes makes it difficult to know which way we are headed with our money. The main point is that money is currency we exchange for things. It is very powerful and certainly means different things to different people at different times in their different lives.

My friend Donna is a negotiator. People need to have the skills or use the skills of a good negotiator so they don't spend too much of their money unwisely. When things go wrong, people don't live up to contracts, or appliances start making weird noises when they are still under warranty, members of my family and I ask ourselves, "What would Donna do?" The woman can be assertive. She can charm folks, question folks, tire folks out, or simply find more attentive folks. In short, Donna can negotiate, and we seek her out to help us learn. Negotiators can save you money. Her husband Dan is in the wholesale flower business, and he is a salesman. In fact, partly due to his work, our little valley is the world's largest distributor of three types of flowers: Larkspur, Delphinium, and Stock. To be the world's largest anything impresses the heck out of me. Salesmen also negotiate, but that is just one part of their repertoire. Salesmen are motivators, joiners, planners, negotiators, and more. If they do all of these things well, and they time it right, they make money. Making money and saving money are behaviors that do not come easily to some folks. Dan and Donna may have some issues that perplex them but they do just fine with money.

Because money is such a force, I would assert that is worth looking at more deeply. The ca-ching sound of the cash register is a powerful symbol to many in my parents' generation. My dad worked in my grandpa's store during the Depression. Hearing the ca-ching was a signal that money was being made, and there would be food on the table. He stayed awake late just to provide food for the table and hearing that sound was very reinforcing.

In my business, the sound of an active fax machine or an arriving e-mail has replaced the ca-ching of the cash register. Even though at one level it means that work is coming in, it also means that our business is growing, and that is, as Martha Stewart would say, a good thing. In the wholesale flower business, my friend Dan just loves to hear the sound of the printer spewing out labels for his orders. In some respects, it sounds just like the old ca-ching.

My daughters do not often discuss money directly. However, they do discuss something they call the "bling." As best I can understand, that has to do with sparkly things, shiny stuff, and lots of other pretty things that inform the world that you have a certain status. Apparently bling is worth the most when someone else gives it to you. I have not witnessed them spending a great deal of what little money they do have to purchase bling. To bridge a generation gap, they want the bling without the ca-ching. I am guessing that there is something in its inessential nature that makes the bling worth more when it shows up at the appropriate time.

Despite my best attempts at refraining from lecturing on the same topics I listened to as a young boy, I do at times lapse. My dad was fond of saying, "I wouldn't have to repeat stuff if you would listen to me the first time." I've even heard those exact words come out of my own mouth. Working hard for the things in life that you want is just one of those ideas I can't resist repeating. Money is to be earned, saved, invested wisely, and not wasted. However, I've also learned another lesson from my ladies, and that is money is to be shared, to be enjoyed, and to be spent. All ca-ching and no bling makes a life dull.

It's Just a Couch

Perhaps the most famous couch in history belonged to a man by the name of Sigmund Freud. To say that he was and is controversial is so understated that if he were still alive today and heard this, he would probably issue that famous Ah Ha. He spent a great deal of time listening to women. He also realized that women are very complex and that sometimes they are willing to share that complexity if you get them in the right position and shut up long enough for them to get to the point. Also, he figured out that if he sat down face-to-face with his patients, they would read things into his reactions that would sometimes take them off course. Over time, Freud settled on a technique in which a woman would lay down on that famous couch while he sat just out of view. He listened a lot, struggled with many issues, and then went about trying to enlighten the other physicians and related healers of his day. If you were to walk into my office today, you would see a replica of that couch—but that is a whole different story.

If you already have a strong opinion of Dr. Freud and his couch and his feelings about women, you are not alone. Along with religion and politics, discussions about sexual behaviors do tend to draw strong opinions. Unfortunately for some, Freud also thought very deeply and wrote in German. The net result of that is that he is someone who most of us have probably heard about or read about but haven't had the time or the inclination to actually read what he wrote. You may not be aware that there are actually "authorized" translations of his work. As that implies, there are many things said about Freud that really irk those who really put some time into studying what he actually said. I did not read all of those translations, but as doctoral candidates, my colleagues and I were asked to read many of them, so I think I can share a few insights, at least about the couch.

Dr. Freud encountered patients who were, like him, products of the Victorian era. Among other disturbing things that happened during that era, there was a lot of repression going on. Women were told they were extremely improper if they had rich, sexual feelings—even after they were married. Worse yet, there was also the strong implication that they might actually burn in hell for their feelings. (As a side note, it is interesting that prostitution flourished during that same queenly era.) Even the undergarments that proper women wore looked painful. All in all, it was not a happy time to be a woman.

Many patients whose symptoms could not be explained very well by the medical knowledge of that time were referred to the good doctor. Women were referred to Freud when their physicians ran out of answers. If someone feels odd or depressed or anxious, and the medical community of our time gets a hold of them, she usually gets pills. In those days, a patient could get ignored, sent to a priest for exorcism, or be recommended a whole host of treatments that today would seem totally unrelated to how the person felt. It is pretty easy to see how Freud's gig got started.

Freud encountered a French hypnotist named Mesmer, who appeared to be able to get folks to do and feel things by making powerful suggestions. I'm sure it looked as mysterious to him, at first, as it does to most people today. That influence combined with Freud's caseload of suffering women and their willingness to talk to him got him thinking about thoughts and the realm of the unconscious—odd things that that doctors can't really see. We can hear how people talk about thoughts and make inferences. We can see how they act and make inferences about how they think. Nowadays, we can even image how someone imagines, but Freud never had access to an MRI.

Freud left the world with a paradigm shift in the way we listen and interpret, and he used a couch to do it. Not all of his ideas have proven to be useful over the years. Some even seem extremely strange in the context of today's culture. However, let me cast a few out there to see if they still float. Some people repress sexual thoughts and images. In other words, something bubbles up from a source where it is hiding, and we have a thought. If that thought is not timed right or not one we can act on, we shove it back down. It doesn't take years on the couch for some folks to see that. Some people are in denial about very real issues that negatively affect their lives. Those folks don't usually look for time on the couch. In fact, they are still running around blaming someone or something else.

Some people project the real causes of their own misery onto other folks. The people who do a lot of projecting may be dropped off for couch time, but they seldom come in on their own. Some, however, at some point want help going really deeply into issues that seem to keep bubbling up. If they have the money and the time and the persistence that it takes, the effort can really pay off.

However, I am not a psychoanalyst. Psychologists come from many schools and many traditions. I have spent some time looking at couches and dealing with trouble between couples, though, and there seems to be a slight connection. It is a bit of a stretch, but follow if you will. You should always keep in mind that even Freud was apt to point out that things don't always have to have deeper meaning, but that they just often do have deeper meanings.

Non-Freudian types of couches are often designed to get folks together. You may have the three-piece traditional sofa or the smaller love seat version. All couches are bigger than one person really needs to have to, say, read or watch TV or knit or just space out. Sleeping is another matter altogether. When someone sleeps on the couch when there is a perfectly good bed elsewhere, that person is either really tired, or there is trouble in that other bedroom. If you sit with two other people on a couch, and you want to talk to all of them, it is not an especially efficient design. Two, however, can manage just fine on the couch. They can even touch and snuggle and do fun things together sharing that space.

If you don't like couches, chances are you have a few chairs. Chairs often have arms, or even if they don't, they are not really good for sharing a space. They seem to work just fine alone, but they can be arranged with others to promote conversation or eating or both. The real difference is that couches invite someone into your physical space in a much more intense way. I'm not implying that a good seating arrangement can't include both. I am, however, aware that not everyone is that comfortable sharing space, even if they are in love with the other person. They might even find it hard to share a very large couch with a loved one, or they might just find it more pleasant to have their own chair. I call these two typologies "couch people" and "chair people."

Couch people sometimes marry chair people, and things can get dicey. To a couch person, sitting on a chair alone when loved ones are around is a sign of something. It seems odd to them, so they feel a need question you about the state of the relationship. To a chair person, the idea of sitting together without clear lines of demarcation, is just plain uncomfortable. Couch people and chair people come in both genders. I have daughters who prefer the couch, and one who is definitely more at ease with a reading chair. As a clinical psychologist I can attest that watching how people choose to arrange themselves in chairs and couches at a family therapy session can tell you a lot about how the session is going to progress. Sometimes, though, a couch is just a place where the dog hangs out when we are not around, and sometimes it is just a couch.

The Colonel Has Red Shoes and a Matching Handbag

I realize that this heading could lead a person toward a whole different direction of the closet, but bear with me for a while. It has nothing to do with gay folks serving their country in the armed forces. It does have to do with women in uniform and the uniforms women wear. I also must confess that I have a special fondness for women in uniform. Perhaps that is too subtle a way of saying that I think they are hot. I married a soldier and was introduced to her by a woman of rank. I do not find the military in general to be especially hospitable to most women, although some manage to do just fine. My late friend Dennis married a nurse. She is an awesome combination of beauty, caring, and often wears a cute little nursing uniform that fits her perfectly. My wife retired recently, and sadly, I have not seen her in her uniform for some time. As of this moment, my good friend Cathy, the colonel who introduced me to my wife, is planning her life after the Air Force. I recently got a note from her, and it started me thinking about what women wear. She has already picked out a pair of red shoes and a matching handbag for her life after the service. I'll bet it brings a smile to her face just thinking about them.

If you join the service, as I did, you come to understand that the uniform is something proper and rigid, and it is very important that you wear it correctly. You are taught how to put it on, how align your shirt and trousers properly, how to spit shine your shoes, and where to put every conceivable award, rank, name tag, or anything else that can be pinned to the jacket. There is, in the military, a right place to wear the right thing. Hats go on at particular times and come off at particular times and places. In basic training, soldiers even learn that uniforms are so important they need special attention in your trunk. Socks are folded so they smile at you. Shirts are hung in precise rows. You get the drift. My tenure with them was brief and relatively uneventful. To use a clothing analogy, the "fit was never just right." However, I did leave with an understanding of what the pressure to dress correctly is all about. Now, some women take to the pressure to

28

dress correctly with ease. Others struggle and resist. It doesn't really matter, though, because if you are in a system that thinks that clothes should look a particular way, then you are going to feel pressure to dress that way.

Psychologists have come to understand the powerful effect of stories. We even have a whole branch for this now called narrative psychology. The concept is ancient, but the effects and uses of narratives are being studied with renewed vigor. Here is an example that relates to red shoes. The story of Dorothy from *The Wizard of Oz* operates on many levels. It tells of a young women's surrealistic flight from her homeland in Kansas due to the massive winds of an inescapable tornado. The story tells of her fellow travelers who seek the great wizard to help them overcome their shortcomings. She endures great hardship and encounters many wicked things and a pretty nasty witch along the way. The short version of one of the most poignant points of the story (keeping in mind that it is usually very unwise to shorten stories in the presence of real narrative psychologists) is that the wizard is a fake. He is a phony who hides behind a great curtain, and Dorothy later exposes him as such. Here is the kicker: a very nice and mysterious good witch lets Dorothy know that she actually has all the power she needs to go home and has had it all along. It's in her ruby slippers! Click those babies together in the right way, and it's back to Kansas for Dorothy!

There is some powerful stuff in that story. Dorothy gets her red shoes by accidentally killing another woman. It's really OK, though, since the witch who gets squished by Dorothy's house was wicked in the first place. Somewhere along the way Dorothy has to kill that woman's sister, too, but again, Dorothy kills her with an accidental melting of sorts because she needed to save her new straw man friend. She learns that men are flawed, and that the really big important ones are often just a lot of hot air and smoke screens. Most importantly, though, she demonstrates for generations to come the power of a great pair of ruby slippers.

There are many more stories that may inadvertently shape our attitudes toward clothing. Cinderella got a rich prince by cramming her feet into tiny glass slippers. I, personally, have always been skeptical that she left the thing behind by accident. James Bond seduced a woman by drinking out of a shoe. Brilliant! However, the real cause probably goes deeper. Women feel pressure to look a particular way, and some will go to extraordinary lengths to meet that demand. We can argue over where that pressure comes from. Many women fault men for just about every inconvenience they face. Conversely, many men blame women for just about every inconvenience they face. But pressure is pressure is pressure.

Clothing can put pressure on all women, not just those in famous tales. One example concerns a statue that the women in my house all love. Some time after the birth of my third and last daughter, I bought a piece of art. It was a sculpture of a whale pushing its calf upward, entitled "First Breath." I did this thing up right. I arranged a viewing room at the gallery. I took my wife there, just to browse. At the right moment, the gallery lights were lowered, the curtain was raised, and the statue was displayed. I asked her if that was something she liked, and she started to cry. It didn't take a PhD in women's studies to see that she really liked the statue. I told her that I had purchased it for her earlier in the day to salute her rearing of our daughter, and she cried some more. We took it home, and it migrates throughout the downstairs of my home depending on the state of the ooze, I suppose, or on some other need she seems to have to move things around.

One day I got home, and draped on this particularly meaningful piece of art was a bra. I'm not making this up. If you don't live with women, you probably don't know as much as you should about this item of apparel. For example, I had always assumed that bras come off last in the upper-body dressing department. In my house, that is simply not the case. Often they are the first item dispensed of when a woman needs some relief from the pressures of the day. If need be, they can pull them out their sleeves, and sometimes they just end up in places they were never intended to be. Now, I know that the women in my house love that sculpture, so I just must assume that relieving the pressure of the bra, at times, takes precedence over art appreciation.

Glass Slippers and Glass Ceilings

I read the story of Cinderella to my daughters when they were small. The story line here is well known and, unfortunately, not unique. Step moms and stepsisters do not come across well. Despite her stepfamily's best efforts at humiliating her, Cinderella gets the fairy godmother's blessings, gets the handsome prince's attention with her grace and stunning good looks, and then rushes out to meet her curfew, inadvertently dropping the famous glass slipper along the way. The prince tracks her down, and they eventually ride off to live happily ever after. Narrative psychologists talk of that scenario as one of the rescue myths. As a father of daughters, I focused less on the subtle messages of the story than on trying my best to encourage reading and imagination. I must admit, however, that my imagination was more focused on the idea that perhaps later in their lives, my daughters might consider dating wealthy men. Some fantasies were just never meant to materialize.

I had this acquaintance once. We both ran small businesses, so there were many reasons and occasions to catch up and chat. In addition to her business, she was devoted to being a spouse, a mother, and an active volunteer in our community. I don't know this for sure, but I presume she spent a good portion of her time juggling the various demands of her life. It had been quite some time since our last chat, but I must confess, the direction her life had taken amazed me. I can only assume that the motivation for this change was something really persuasive, something like some man saying, "Oh, this is not really a subject that women understand." I don't know if he was trying to sell her something or impress her with something, but I am sure that he wasn't successful taking that approach.

Sometimes dads are underestimated, and sometimes we are overestimated. I have had personal experiences with both. People have brought me things to fix, as if that were a part of my genetic endowment. I can fix some things, but I prefer to put a value on my time first and judge how that relates to the cost of buying replacement things. People have also assumed I was incompetent with babies simply because I was a man. I must admit that the former situation amused me, but the latter aggravated me a bit.

Some of the women I know frequently face being underestimated, and it can generate a lot of resentment at times. I am pretty sure this particular lady was not amused that someone implied that market forces and investing were just too complex for her to fathom. Or, at the very least, to fathom in ways that greatly exceeded what this particular man understood. Men are fiercely competitive about a lot of things. In some respects, they are even evaluated based upon this drive to compete. On the other side for women, if you live in a time and culture that gives opportunities and tells you to dream and to rise up, it really hits hard when you bump into glass ceilings.

Whatever the reason, this woman decided to tackle the issue of investing. She read, studied, and attended seminars. She consulted experts, read more books, and sifted through the information. Over time, her language changed: stunning portfolios were no longer fashion accessories; portfolios were built on asset allocation formulas that made sense to her in a profound way. She based her current formula on "Modern Portfolio Theory," an impressive set of principles designed at MIT to maximize return and minimize risk.

Pigs used to be things that lived in sties and snorted. Now, for my friend, pork bellies had futures. The values of futures can fluctuate wildly. If you know a great deal about the future of pigs from the supply and demand side, there is serious money to be made. If not, there is also serious money to be lost. She went from being able to time markets by reading the signs on their doors to realizing the futility of market-timing strategies. She traded one world for another, and she loved it.

Shopping for a hat used to be something that made her happy. Now large caps have stability, and small caps have volatility. I know that my friend made a lot of money in her journey. I do not know if she later lost just as much because we have not spoken in years. Market forces do tend to fluctuate like that. I do know that if she called me with a tip, it would be worth my time to look into it. I also learned a lot from this woman and tried to share that with my own women.

Different people think different ways about financial issues, and the way a person thinks about these issues can determine his or her future. I don't know as much about finance as many people do who spend their lives investing and helping others invest. I have, however, learned a few things that I think warrant sharing. All my children really love this diatribe, so I thought I would write part of it down for those who may not get to hear it themselves. Actually, the first response from my children when I go down this road is to nod, roll a few eyes, and try to change the subject. First and foremost, never tell people that they cannot come to understand something. Never allow yourself to be trapped by thinking that there is something you cannot do. It is far better to frame the issue in your mind as something you have not learned to do or something you have not devoted the time to understand. Similar to the world of fashion, in investing, a little knowledge can be a dangerous thing. A glass slipper may be in, but it doesn't fit everyone, and it can't be comfortable in the long run.

Fortunately, some women and some men know a lot about investing. Also, most people at least know that they can get more stuff or work less time if they come to understand the world of money more completely. Unfortunately, one of the major ways that people take advantage of others is by selling schemes that do not make good financial sense. It is often said, but it bears repeating, that if something seems too good to be true, it most likely is. High rewards usually bring high risks. There is risk in not risking, but people do vary greatly in their tolerance for financial risk.

The Cliffs Notes version of the road map to financial success usually involves the concepts of diversification and discipline. It takes discipline to start investing early and to plan for the future. It takes some time to really understand the power of compound interest, both on the spending side and on the earning side. Not only does it take discipline to plan the work, but it also takes a fair amount of discipline to work the plan. People tend to think of diversification in too narrow a way. Paying down debt and looking outside of the stock market for diversification is also important. There are plenty of professed gurus who were really just lucky and were in the right places at the right times. All of us who bought a house a few decades ago are not geniuses; some of us were just looking for a good place to live.

In the end, a good plan must address the fundamental concept of success. To me, that means having enough to do or buy what you have decided you want to do or buy, for however long you have left. To do that, you need to know what you have, which is not quite as simple as it sounds. You also need to know how much you will need and how much time you have left to accumulate that amount. There are people whose lives are devoted to predicting how much time you have left. As cold as it may sound, the insurance industry does not just about protect your loved ones. There is money to be made and lost depending on how good they are at predicting your demise. Formulas can project what you will probably need, but formulas are just tools.

The real issue involves deciding what you want. If the answer to that question is something like, "I want as much as I can get," then you will never attain success. You can't know how much you can get until your life is already over. Sadly, even then there are bills remaining to be paid. If the answer is something like "I just want as much as I deserve," you will never consider yourself successful. Money doesn't play fair. Sometimes you get more than you deserve and sometimes less. It doesn't always reflect your self-worth or what you think you deserve.

I can imagine that it really hurts to hit a glass ceiling. I can also imagine that it hurts to cram your foot into a glass slipper just to get to a dance where you hope to meet someone who will make all your problems magically go away. But we live in the real world, and sometimes things made of glass just need a good hammer. In one sense, the best hammer here is a good financial plan. There are many metaphorical hammers that are not good, and it is a challenge to learn the difference. Financial plans can and probably should change over time. They are not perfect, but they do increase the odds of getting what you want in life.

If you are like most people, your honest answer to the question of what you want is less clear than you would like. You may be confused about how assets are valued and how they are accumulated. There is certainly plenty of confusion inherent in the process of understanding how assets might be more or less likely to grow. If someone tries to convince you that they know it all and that you don't need to know, kick them with your best glass slippers.

Food-a-tudes

Legends tell us that our attitudes toward food used to be quite simple. Men killed it, women gathered it and cooked it, and they both ate as much of it as they could. If they were good at the process, they might even share some with the kinfolk. I imagine that if the women were not available, due to the remoteness of the hunt, let's say, then the men would fire up the pit, gather some intoxicants to chew, smoke, or drink, and roast the meat themselves. Somehow things changed over the eons, and we are left to deal with food-a-tudes. A food-a-tude is not an eating disorder. Eating disorders are nasty things that cause serious problems. People, usually women, can die from some eating disorders. Food-a-tudes are simply attitudes surrounding food, which I believe warrant discussion.

I have this colleague, a nice, professional woman who is also a great cook. Every Christmas season she wears a pin that says "He sees you when you're eating." Now, I get the joke. Santa knows when you are naughty and when you are nice. He even keeps a list and checks it twice to make sure he gets his assessment correct. But the message here is deeper. Women develop food-a-tudes that surround being watched and judged about eating. This nice little pin is just another reminder that it doesn't matter if you sneak it late at night, eat salad on the date and then go for the Häagen-Dazs after he leaves, or whatever; you will be caught. Ouch.

The message is everywhere. If you shop at grocery stores, you can't even get through the checkout line without being bombarded with input on the costs of ignoring the plague of overeating. Even the tabloid news sources that report alien abductions and six-headed babies are in on the plot. They love to catch a movie star or famous person in an odd pose that shows that they actually have real bodies—and that some of them even have cellulite. Heaven forbid we should age! New diets hit the magazines, and skinny models look amazingly happy to have managed to lose some extraordinary amount of weight in some ridiculously short period of time. So you go for food, and you get guilt and diets.

I must confess something before I go on. In psychology, for a while, there was a great tendency to blame the family, and mothers in particular, for everything. If they were too quick or too strict with toilet training, they reared anal-retentive people. If, however, they were too slow to get the task done, their children would become messy folks. And Heaven forbid they weaned too early or late! Those notions don't hold with most of us anymore, but as far as food-a-tudes are concerned, it starts with the family. My own particular "family of origin," as we call it, is of the southern flavor. Mom's folks were from North Carolina, and my dad's were settled in the great state of Alabama. We moved a lot when my siblings and I were kids, but we always managed to have hog jowl and black-eyed peas at New Year's. I have tasted parts of beasts that most people in my current location would never dream were meant for human consumption. My mom was far more interested in politics, her church, and the welfare of the less fortunate than in cooking, but she is a wonderful cook.

Partially as a result of this conditioning, I love southern women. My Aunt Becky and her cow-pasture-walking sisters were Ya-Yas long before the book came out. I completely understand what would drive a woman to want to become a Sweet Potato Queen. I even married a southern girl, the former Miss Jacksonville, Arkansas. She smiled at me and said "Hey" instead of the customary "hello" when we first met. She and her sister, who, by the way, talk to each other all the time, still say "y'all." They even use the plural form of that phrase, which I heard a radio comedian poke fun at as if it were improper, "all y'all." When I first saw her, she had paid some attention to her hair, and her lips were very red. I did not for one minute underestimate the fact that beneath all that charm there was a really strong woman. She lives with me in California, but she is still of the South. If you were to visit us, she would make sure you felt welcome, and you would get a great hug on the way in and on the way out.

When I visit the South, one of my favorite things to do is eat. Once I visited a little place in Alabama called the Lean-To Café and munched on "wangs." I swear to you, that is not only how it was pronounced, but that is how it was spelled on the menu. My wife took me to a spot in Little Rock where the junior portion of fried catfish had four full filets, coleslaw, garlic bread and French fries. Another day, we shot down a couple dozen oysters at a bar, with drinks, and got change back from our $20. Those were fun times.

The southern women that I know are a fairly diverse lot. Some have very little inclination to cook. However, most that I have known have several qualities that I really admire. The first is that at their core, they recognize that to many men, college football is not "just a game." They may appreciate it, or they may not, but they understand the passion. My dad and siblings are Auburn folks. Travel to Alabama some autumn day, and you will sense what southern women are steeped in throughout their lives. Religion and politics are subjects that can cause decent folks to turn, but football in Alabama is still the king. Another thing I have witnessed is that, even if they don't do it anymore, most know how to fry a chicken and make biscuits. If you are lucky enough, they even put ham inside the biscuit or gravy over the biscuit—and that is great stuff!

Here is a chicken-frying screening test that is a quick, easy, and foolproof way to help you see if you are attached to someone who understands this aspect of food. If you watch someone pull the skin off the pieces of fried chicken and frown, they don't pass the test. If they only buy select portions of white meat or mention anything that hints of the free-range conditions of the fowl prior to its appearance at the grocery store, they don't pass. If, however, they know the secrets of soaking things in buttermilk, something of the mysteries of spicing, and a bit about how hot the oil has to be, you are on the right track.

I must admit that some go too far. My mother-in-law, who spent a good deal of her life on a farm in Arkansas, fries corn. I am not kidding. She takes it right off the best natural delivery device a vegetable ever had and slaps it into a hot pan of butter and brown sugar. Sad thing is, it tastes great. You can even fry a Twinkie, and you can certainly fry a turkey. You might just be curious as to why, if I am so enamored with Southern women, I headed west to California as soon as the military saw fit to let me go. It is really no mystery at all. In late high school, I lived briefly near Santa Barbara in a small town called Lompoc. The weather is awesome. Now I live there permanently, and I am really comfortable. I can play golf year-round if my back holds up, but when they serve me tea, it does not come sweet. For those unfortunate readers who may not be so enlightened, tea in the South comes either as "regular" (a fair amount of sugar added) or "unsweetened". Another sad thing is that women here are bombarded with food-a-tudes. As a whole, this healthy eating obsession also keeps men around longer, which may or may not be such a good plan.

My wife and I eat Thai food, Italian food, and Chinese food. We have even come to like sushi. However, when my wife speaks of frying chickens it is always in the past tense. As in; something she used to do before she learned that you can buy it if you really need to, and it is really not healthy for you and it really upsets your stomach these days, so why do you even bother eating it…You get the drift. Now, she still makes a mean biscuit, but the gravy just isn't happening.

Eat with women long enough and you might even encounter some who eat on smaller plates just to feel as if they are getting a full portion of something. My in-laws drove out from Arkansas one fall and parked their giant motor home right in front of our house. They plugged it in, leveled it off, and settled in for a nice visit. After eating with us for many meals and thanking us each and every time for the fine food, our hospitality, and all the rest, my mother-in-law finally asked in desperate tones if we could perhaps use real-size dinner plates. That struck me as fine idea.

I don't intend to demean other cultures or other regions, as I have had only limited exposure to them. I have had some, though, so I feel I can make an assertion or two, but these should not be considered facts—more like subjective observations.

One of my first roommates in college was a man named Elliot, who just happened to be Jewish and just happened to come from Miami. He had a full head of curly, dark hair and never lacked for female attention. Being away from my family, I had the pleasure of traveling to his home and dining with his family. Elliot's mom was incredible. When she did our laundry, which by itself was a fine gesture, she ironed our underwear. I had never had that done to my boxer shorts in my life, before or since. She went out in the morning and brought home fresh bagels, which she lathered up with cream cheese and topped with capers and smoked salmon. What a way to start the day! When it came time to eat lunch, she asked us what we would like and then proceeded to shop at these places that were Kosher and fresh, and I think she genuinely loved the process. We got steak for lunch. I am not kidding. Each of us got our custom-ordered steak for lunch. I wanted to be in Elliot's world for a while.

Unfortunately, Organic Chemistry and Elliot did not agree, and after he left school to return home, I lost touch with him. I can only imagine that it must be a lot of fun and a lot of pressure, for some, to be around food when you're Jewish.

It seems to involve, lots of laws, tons of tradition, and even a small amount of guilt. Food-guilt in particular, since, after all, it was eating that forbidden apple that kicked off the whole mess. Most importantly, I cannot imagine that most women would find the idea of caring for Elliot the way his mom did, a pleasant thought to endure..

My next roommate's family came from Cuba. They were wonderful folks who lived in Tampa, Florida. I got to spend a Thanksgiving meal with them and loved it, but they did have some issues around food that would probably cause some folks to take a second look. For starters, the women cooked it, served it, cleaned up after it, and then ate somewhere else in the house. But the food itself was awesome. We had lasagna, talked politics, drank sangria, watched football, ate some turkey, ate more lasagna, drank some more sangria, and then I think I feel asleep on their couch. They were warm and hospitable, great cooks and great eaters. But I have to think that at some point, the women are considering leaving the kitchen. When they do, I can imagine there will be food-a-tudes aplenty.

Not all women have food-a-tudes, but the ones that don't are less common than you might suspect. I saw this scene once in a movie, the title of which escapes me at present, but I do recall it vividly. A man and a woman are sitting opposite each other at a table. The server plops down a succulent array of shellfish and melted butter. This woman, without waiting, without guilting, and without paying attention to anything else, proceeds to dig in. She cracks crab legs open and dips the contents into the melted butter. Not partway but all the way up to her lovely fingers. She then sucks every last morsel into her beautiful lips and pays absolutely no attention to the butter that is now dribbling down her face. At some point, she does remember that she is not alone. She smiles coyly at her dining partner and then returns to devouring her food. Now, if that movie scene disgusts you, you may have a few latent food-a-tudes yourself. If not, you may just get what I am trying to point out.

I have not visited France, or anywhere else in Europe, but I plan to. When I do, one of the things I am going to try to do is understand how they manage to avoid food-a-tudes, if in fact they really do. I hear they enjoy fabulous food without guilt. Bon appétit!

Divine Cat Herding

In the South, there is a way of talking that is often infused with the phrase "God bless." The nicest part is that you can just fill in your own beginning or ending and still have a really nice thought. "God bless" those ladies for helping out at the church dinner. "God bless" the soldiers that are keeping us safe. I am really proud to be an American, and may "God bless." It is sometimes shortened to just "Bless you." That shortened version can be a sentence unto itself, acknowledging your special place ("Bless you"), or sometimes it just follows a sneeze, in which case the emphasis changes to "*Bless* you." It can even be used to dismiss you in a very genteel way, as if to say, "Well, may God bless you anyway."

You know that a phrase is sacred in the South when it gets to precede a kickoff. As in, "May God bless the players today, as they knock themselves silly just so that we can share a few brews. And, if it is your will, Lord, for the next twelve months we can witness to your glory by demonstrating our inherent superiority over those Crimson Tide ne'er-do-wells, which of course we will do with the utmost humility, as you have commanded." OK, I never actually heard that in my own home, but at times we did hear things that implied that God really did smile on certain football teams, especially the Auburn team.

I am here to bear witness that God may indeed bless those that take the care and trouble to coach our kids as they are developing. I am not referring to those that get paid, or those that do it because they want their own kid to learn from the best possible teacher around, themselves. Lord knows I am not referring to the ones that do it so they can work out their own competitive or athletic shortcomings through the lives of their poor children; as a psychologist, I can attest to the fact that issues like those are real and do mess kids up.

I am referring to those that volunteer their time—and it takes lots of time—to help kids learn how to play organized sports. They go to meetings, make calls, and sacrifice their afternoons and weekends, all to help kids learn how to play, to compete, to work together as a team, to sacrifice, and to play a role that may not be a starting one but that is still an important one, all in an effort to help the team.

Oh, and they also have to deal with other parents. If you have ever done that, you can attest to the fact that it is not always fun. Bless them all.

I love watching my own daughters play. I have been fortunate enough to have sufficient occupational flexibility to allow me to watch them many, many times. I have sponsored teams, been "Team Dad" (this means you get to set up and enforce the snack schedule and take the banner to games, among other things), and even been coerced into coaching my own team, for a too-brief period of time. My special blessing was to coach adolescent and pre-adolescent girls, in basketball and soccer. In fact, that was the inspiration for the title of this particular homily.

Many young ladies love sports. Like all things in life, some come by that naturally, and some acquire the taste. My friend's daughter Dominique actually plays collegiate water polo at a very high level. If you are not familiar with that sport, it involves a great deal of endurance and enough underwater fighting to make a boxing fan cringe. Sports provide a unique venue where dads, moms, sisters, brothers, sons, daughters, and even ex-jocks without kids can all come together to do something positive. There are teams to be selected, schedules to be made, coaches to be recruited, leagues to manage, fields to set up and take down, uniforms to buy and clean, assorted knee pads to keep track of, banners to announce your chosen name and to rally your fan support. And most importantly, for my young teams, there were Snack Moms. Hallelujah and pass the Gatorade and chocolate-covered granola.

Sponsoring is easy, and it usually involves just writing a check or two and deciding whether your last name is too long to inflict on any team's weekly news dispatch. Running a league is in a whole different category. That is a difference in scale somewhat akin to the difference between going to Mass and running the diocese. It is the difference between buying coffee for the homeless guy on the pier and living the life of Mother Teresa. OK, that might be a stretch, but in any event, we need to stop and bless those who do that particular part of the process, both the men and the women. My friends Roger, Scott, and Sharon have each done all or parts of that league-running task. They are just a few of the thousands who carry out that task. Bless them.

Coaching is just one part of the process, but it is a very visible part and a very interesting challenge. If you have not coached girls, you may not know this, but they really do like to win. They can also be incredibly tough, if the motivation is right. Most of the time, coaching is really fun, and the kids really seem to be in sync with each other. You select teams, hold practices, meet neat kids and neat parents, play exciting games, ice down an occasional sprain, pass out awards, and get a priceless picture that captures that process and labels you as "Coach." Good stuff.

Sometimes, however, things can go terribly awry. A parent does not think you quite understand their daughter's unique gifts. Another mom or dad decides that trophies should not to be awarded if the team does not go far enough in the post-season tournament. Another parent becomes convinced that the volunteer referee is deliberately ignoring the brutal fouling of their princess, and wasn't anyone aware that they just spent $5,000 at the orthodontist to insure that their child's smile would be just perfect?

The parents are not always the instigators. Sometimes a girl might decide that you do not understand how vitally important her boyfriend is to her life. Another hears an opponent using words that clearly were meant to degrade, humiliate, or at the worst instigate a physical response that would chill most men. Another more casual player decides that the offense just doesn't suit her style of play, and the uniform doesn't fit right anyway, so it must be time to phone a friend who will at least pretend to understand how serious that can be. I am not necessarily suggesting that Satan is involved. However, it is probably a mistake to rule out any possible cause of the diversion. I can offer witness to this: that when those types of forces combine, you can lose control of the entire congregation.

Through divine providence, our family was called to Atlanta, Georgia, in 1996. We watched with reverence as Mia Hamm and her teammates took on the world. We sat among many nations and made joyful noises as those women kicked—well, you know what they kicked. Let me attempt to phrase that in a more succinct and more appropriate way: God bless the 1996 US women's Olympic soccer team.

Having borne witness to the ultimate woman's team, it is no exaggeration to say that the games I coached bore no resemblance at all to the games the US Olympic team played. In fact, if you are old enough to remember those old magnetic games that you turned on and all the players kind of jiggled in similar directions, which would be closer to what you might have seen if you were in the blimp above any of the fields where my young girls played.

I love dogs, and I appreciate cats. Domestic canines are very much interested in pleasing you, in establishing and obeying the strongest members, in playing a role in getting themselves food, and when the mood hits, in scratching what itches. You may think of that as crude, but it is actually just a truism. If it itches, scratching feels really good. Canines also, by nature, hunt in packs. I am well aware that boys have difficulty learning to channel their competitive drives into team efforts. However, I have not had that challenge and will defer that discussion to those who have.

Cats are also fine hunters and do interesting things to small objects that dangle. However, if you throw nine cats into a field with one mouse, they will all converge at once, with no thought of what the other cats are doing. It does not matter if the old guy on the sidelines is yelling instructions about where they should be while the mouse is running. They may even win and strut their prize home and bat it around and practice with it. But it is not about what position they were in when the mouse got caught. Cats are beautiful, cunning, and graceful. Most cats, however, are not easy to herd.

Can I get an *Amen*?

Mo' Money

Psychologists who study family systems report that we get a lot of our issues about money from our families. I would not disagree. For my part, my dad was a product of the Depression and was fanatical about teaching us kids the value of money. It is a true story and one that I have repeated to my own kids, that my dad actually charged me mileage to borrow the car for my prom night. After all, the sooner I learned that money didn't grow on trees and that driving costs far more than just the price of gas, the better.

Mom has Quaker religious roots. In that tradition, learning not to waste, boast, or be showy is deeply important. My father has passed on, but to this day my mom has a fundamental dislike of all things "wasteful." Whenever she leaves after a too-brief visit, we will find tucked away in our refrigerator, small portions of what she refers to as "perfectly good meals for later." If you cook too much food or buy too big a house or even shop at large bulk stores, it just makes her uncomfortable.

When I was a young man of about nineteen, I stopped taking money from my folks. I phrase it that way to emphasize the fact that they were perfectly able and willing to give it to me, provided I did certain things. That was not an equation that sat well with me at that time of my life. I had the classic imbalance between confidence in what I knew and actual knowledge. As some still do, I chose a different school in a far away state to start my education. I left home with one suitcase, one large trunk, and a head full of wrong thoughts, but tons of confidence; I must have made my parents chuckle. Fortunately for me, the Air Force helped with the costs, and jobs were not that hard to locate at the time.

One thing that happens to many of us as we get older is that we start to realize certain truths about the world that at one point our parents tried unsuccessfully to tell us. In short, you find yourself delivering the same talks they gave you, over and over and over—the talks you swore you would never give anyone. In our younger years, we are pretty convinced that our parents are simply out of touch.

Nice folks at times, but in no way connected to today's world. As we grow older, it becomes apparent that the nice younger folks we associate with are terribly naïve. Here are some things that I suspect my children will say to theirs, if they are so blessed as to have children of their own.

Money does not, in fact, grow on trees. It usually has to be earned. Sad as that may seem, in most cases that means that it has to be acquired through work. It might be awarded by fiat or by association, but you can't just pick however much you need and go back to playing. Most often, money has strings attached. You may not like that, but that won't change the fact that even if they are not immediately visible, the strings are there. Plastic money is dangerous, due to the mathematical facts of compound interest. And here is the really hard part to swallow: money doesn't play fair.

If you understand money, you will realize that it is neither especially fair nor especially stable. At times it may work out that a particular transaction operates equitably, but, like the universe itself, money is not always a fair system. To make matters worse, the value of things is constantly in flux. In other words, knowing the value of a dollar is important, but the lessons are not simple, and they don't hold still.

In any given month, I employ about 80 people. This makes the business I started one of a large group in this country often called small businesses. I would call my business relatively successful. It is successful in the sense that we provide a good service and decent wages and benefits, and have been around for some time. The relative part is trickier. You will not find us listed anywhere in the *Fortune* 500. I'm pretty sure that you would not find us in the *Fortune* 5,000,000. However, the business does just fine, and I have reached the point where, although I cannot retire, I am tired, and I dream about that day often.

Lots of people start a small business, but unfortunately most do not survive for long. There is just a whole lot to be thought about and a whole lot that can go wrong. Among the things that crash most of those soaring entrepreneurial spirits is a disconnection with the whole issue of money. People who want to start businesses often have a passion for something, like food, or serving autistic children, or building sports cars, but they do not think through all the aspects of turning that passion into a business. They launch the venture well before they have visualized all the steps. The crucial step that is often overlooked or just assumed is that at some point along the way they need to take in more than they pay out. The polite term for what usually happens is "undercapitalization." More simply stated, they don't have enough money or credit to get through what it takes to get things going.

In academia, you get a salary. You may very well have other sources of income, but by and large you are on salary. Teachers usually are not paid in proportion to what they do; it is my opinion that vast majority are actually undervalued. That does not mean that some aren't slacking. It just means that teachers' work is extremely important, and the money is not all that great. People enter that profession for many reasons; they majored in something that had few vocational outlets other than teaching, they liked coaching and they were forced to teach, they did well in college, came back to do research and were forced to teach, and some even had exposure to a great educator and wanted others to have that experience. There are lots of different motivations, but on the whole, the vacation schedules are predictable, and salaried positions are very good for providing stability.

In other areas, though, there is a more direct connection between how well you work and how much money you accumulate. This is one of the factors that drove me to venture into the business world, and I am grateful for the lesson it taught me. In general, businesspeople understand the idea of the food chain. Money and the things it brings are up for grabs, and people are constantly grabbing for yours. It also can consume you just as much as, if not more than, grading essays late at night. But the smarter you do your work in business, the more money you can make, and that seems like a nice contingency to people like me who have an overabundance of confidence.

Employees are generally grateful to have work but are often confused that more money is not automatically associated with more time on the job. Most employees really like fair systems, but it is not always easy to operate fairly and treat your employees fairly in a world that is not always fair. We do try, but sometimes we just have to reinforce talent. In other words, we will pay more simply because someone is blessed with a certain skill set that makes our business work. That is not fair, and it may feel bad, but it does help the bottom line. As if that were not enough to deal with, competitors are often looking at how they can take parts of what you have built and turn it into their own business.

Now let's look at the hardest issue. Let's say you have decided to opt out of the money-earning world, but you are not yet ready to opt out of the spending world. You may do this for any number of noble reasons. A family, a village, or a society needs to have lots of roles filled. Caring for children, caring for the less-abled, or caring for the elderly can be a full-time job. Or you may do this for other, less noble, reasons. The trouble usually comes when the spending world and the earning world get out of synch. When those two worlds get disconnected, ugly things will come out. The power of money is used in unwise ways, spending becomes retribution, and arguments get layers that would confuse a skilled law-yer. Without frequent and direct communication, these discussions can lead to fights, which can escalate into feuds, which become wars, which can ultimately result in the serious thought of taking a buzz saw to the house so that each person will get their half. Of course, that is not my experience, but I have heard of such things.

Special Moms

There are different degrees of knowledge, and I believe there are even different levels of knowing. For example, before the birth of my first child people would caution me that I was not prepared for the life-changing event that was to come. I knew they were right, but I only knew it in my head. From the moment of birth, through the transition home, and well into a few sleepless nights, I began to *know* it in my heart, as well. I received a similar warning about adolescence. I knew that my sweet girls would someday change, but I didn't *know* it until it happened. I now *know* a few things about adolescence.

You may be of the opinion that all moms are special. I've certainly heard that, but I just don't see things that way. To me, to be special implies that someone is unique. To be unique, a person can't be just like everyone else. You may be wondering if I am ignoring special dads, but I am not. There are many special dads, and I don't believe that all dads are special, either. To me the category of "special parents" belongs to the group that remains engaged in the process of parenting children with special needs.

I also need to share that, as a man, I do not cry with ease or with comfort. I do cry; it just doesn't feel the same for me as it seems to feel for the women in my life. Those ladies will actually seek out a "good cry." I have even seen them on the couch together, tissues all around, watching a movie that made them cry last year. They laugh, cry, cry-laugh, sob, and generally report loving the experience. As a matter of course in my daily life, I try to avoid those things that are so powerful that they make me break down and cry. I don't know how you will react to what follows, but it was very hard for me to write.

My colleagues and I see about 1,000 families annually that have members with what are called developmental disabilities. Developmentally disabled people are those who have profound delays in many areas of their cognitive, social and behavioral repertoires. These delays arise in childhood and are likely to persist through their entire life. Some common examples include those with Down's syndrome, mental retardation, and those with autism. (Officially we now referred to them as having autism spectrum disorders to emphasize the range of abilities and disabilities these people possess). I have been engaged in the process of trying to assist the families of the developmentally disabled for close to thirty years. Over the course of that time, I have met some very special moms.

The very first family I encountered in this way had a son with Down's syndrome, who had been subjected to many painful medical procedures. As a result of this, he would resist anything medical—and it is not an understatement to assert that he could resist very powerfully. Our task was to gradually desensitize him, so that regular doctors and dentists could do their work. Over time we did just that, and I *knew* that this would be my field.

I also came to know his mother, Lucia. Lucia really wanted to be a mom. She had waited until the time was right, and she had planned and planned. During the pregnancy she fell and broke her arm and would not allow her doctors to administer any pain medication. Lucia was focused on her son's health, and she was not going to take any chances.

Moms falling down while pregnant do not cause Down's syndrome. It is caused by a fetus having an extra twenty-first chromosome. Down's syndrome kids have unique features that make them easy to recognize. They also have unique medical concerns that often need special attention as they grow and develop. Down's syndrome can be and often is diagnosed prenatally by a process known as amniocentesis. It is also not a diagnosis that is controversial; although that doesn't mean that it is an easy thing to accept. Lucia, however, was at peace.

As I began my own process of understanding how complex life is in this special world, I asked Lucia how she coped. She told me the following story: she had come to understand that special kids have a guaranteed place in Heaven. She believed that God sends them down to earth to live among us. She was given the special task of caring for and loving that little angel. The tasks were hers, and they gave her life great meaning. You may or may not relate to that story, but I was moved, to say the least.

In psychology, there is attention to the fact that grief occurs in cycles. Elisabeth Kubler-Ross wrote about these cycles eloquently in her book *On Death and Dying*. When your own child has a profound illness or disability, it causes a similar cycle. My first grandson was only granted twenty days on earth. When we received news of that, I refused to believe it. Then I tried to investigate whether there was a way to escape the truth; then I got angry. As the reality set in, I cried, and eventually I cried less. To this day, the sight of a small coffin will make me choke. I am thankful that Lucia gave me her wisdom. Now I *know* that my baby grandson Nicholas is resting peacefully in Heaven.

Some disabilities are not evident quite so early. Some become evident as other children start to talk and yours don't. Some when other children start reading and yours struggle. Those that are hard to see immediately often present unique challenges of their own. In the beginning, our periods of denial are may be longer lasting. It is often harder to convince others once we do realize that something is wrong. There are even those who want us to believe that we are complaining too much or that it must be something that we are doing wrong as parents. Trust me, parents in general, and moms by default, carry enough guilt without any help whatsoever.

Medical conditions and disabilities are not all the same. There are tremendous differences in the tolls they take and the challenges they pose for families. It is a mistake to generalize too far about a particular family's struggle simply because of something you have studied or witnessed. Children on the autism spectrum also vary greatly, as do children with reading disabilities, medical conditions, and other mental health problems.
However, there are some similar experiences that many families seem to go through.

There is a period of denial. You don't see things all at once. Then there is a period of confusion. You may hear words that are vaguely familiar, but you still are not sure what that has to do with your child. You hear contradictory things, like "They will grow out of it" or "You need to do something immediately." Or "You are overreacting, here" or "You are not reacting enough." You do your best to provide for your child at home, and you rely on doctors and professionals to help. You also begin a life-long struggle to find answers. At some point, your child reaches school age, and you face a whole different set of hurdles. You meet some incredible professionals and some incredible un-professionals along the way. Every five to ten years, someone publishes a miraculous cure that you leap towards, only to find it not-so-miraculous. Through it all, you are joined by other moms and dads on that same journey.

I know what it feels like to try to convince a doctor or a school system that something needs to be done. I have sat on both sides of the IEP table and liked neither. The IEP, or Individualized Educational Plan, is supposed to improve the odds of children getting the help that they need in school. It often feels like a bitterly contested paper-compliance episode. My own family finally got our most bitter taste of an IEP when our daughter was in third grade and still not reading. We had been ignored, told we were overly concerned, told that kids grow out of reading problems, told that the school districts don't have funding before that age, and completely exhausted before we even got going. At one point, a psychologist even turned to me and asked, "Have you considered reading to her at home?" I could have punched him and probably should have. If you have never had to argue for your child's inclusion in a regular classroom, or even that he or she may need to take more time on a test, you can still know the struggle. If you have been through it, you *know* it.

If you are like our family, you also try all sorts of programs outside the school. You hire tutors; you consult local professionals and hire them to consult. If you live in a small town like we do, you drive to larger towns after school and during the summer to try out their programs. We were learning skills, but they were not fluent enough to get success in school. Issues of persistence and generalization were becoming major points of discussion at dinner when other families might have been discussing the weather. I even went as far as opening my own school, to get a better understanding of the differences between demonstrating mastery of a task (like scoring a high percent on an un-timed recognition test) and becoming fluent in skill development (like being able to blend sounds rapidly enough to actually read with comprehension). It was a fascinating and frustrating journey.

I have also consulted with many school systems and met some wonderful teachers and administrators. Their world is incredibly complex and demanding. They are faced with the task of trying to match the multiple needs of students with the limited resources that they have at their disposal. They do it day in and day out, and it is tough. My only hope is that we continue to nurture the relationships between those folks and our families and children. There are times when those relationships could use a big hug, or at least a cup of coffee and a thank-you note.

One of the most perplexing, complicated, and profound challenges facing us all today is the explosion in the number of children with what are known as autism spectrum disorders. Recent estimates from the Centers for Disease Control put that number as high as 1 in 166 children. Extrapolate that out to your town's population, and you will get a sense of how many moms and dads are dealing with some really major issues. ASD kids do not arrive in the delivery room with a diagnosis. In fact, it takes a few years in most cases, for all the symptoms to become apparent to the right people. That is not to say that these special moms have not been alerting folks for a long time that something was not right with their kid's development; most of the ones I know have. The causes are still being investigated. The treatments emerging remain confusing to understand and difficult to actually locate. Kids with classic symptoms can display really tough behavioral challenges. To complicate the matter further, the classic symptoms involve the child's difficulties with communication and a lack of social responsiveness. Those together make for a very challenging puzzle.

When the diagnosis does not occur until later in the child's life and the treatments are costly and confusing, there is much to be done. My experience with these special moms has taught me many things. First, they love their children in profound ways, despite the extreme challenges they face. Second, they are tremendously diverse. Some are still in denial. Some others are shopping for doctors on a global scale. Some are angry at "the system," and most are tired. Some are focused, energetic, involved, and caring. Most are all of the above at different points in the year. I understand the cycle, but it does present itself differently at different times.

Having to struggle to get folks aligned with the work that needs to be done on behalf of our children is perhaps the greatest struggle. The work is challenging, resources are limited, and ignorance abounds. To make matters worse, the treatments we seek often oversell the results they produce. I don't think they do this on purpose, but it can sure cost a lot in time and money.

I am constantly being asked about cures, and my feeling is this: I do not honestly know how far we can get with each child. I have a good sense of the things we need to be working on and how we need to go about that work. How far each person gets in life or how much time they have to get there is not in my hands. I give that one up. I also know that the sooner we get started with the work and the more we can work together, the better off we will all be. My favorite recent quote is from a young African boy who was suffering from a devastating disease. Despite that illness his words, his determination and his courage, managed to inspire many of us. Young Nkosi Johnson said, "Do all that you can, with what you have, in the time that you have, in the place where you are."

In closing, I will share with you something that I really do *know*. When my own two learning disabled daughters crossed over the stage of our local community college, degrees in hand, I have never been more proud of them or of anything in my life.

Busy Watching Football

At this precise moment, I am busy writing this final chapter. If I am lucky enough at some other point in time, you will be busy reading this work. No one is forcing me to do this, although there has been a lot of chatter around the house about projects that somehow have never quite been finished. If you had placed a call to my main office on the date when I wrote this, they would tell you that I am, officially at least, "on vacation." In truth, the decision to be busy writing is mine. Hopefully, the decision to be busy reading this is your own. Surely those who are living around us will recognize how truly busy we are. Or maybe they won't.

There was a classic moment in our last presidential debates when the incumbent was questioned about some alleged deficiency in his administration. His response was to repeat several times that he "was working hard." He even went a step further and added that "it is hard work, working hard." Your reading of this chapter might be a more immediate example of the dilemma I am trying to highlight. If there is other work going on around you (food being prepared, a lawn being mowed, bills being paid), the folks doing that work might not necessarily understand that you are, in fact, busy reading. To further complicate the situation, if you were reading this as part of a course that I happen to be teaching, you could claim that you were studying, which, of course, sounds much busier than just "reading." I think that sums up a lot of what is going on in our culture today. Everyone seems to be busy, but often they do not seem to be busy doing the things we necessarily want them to be doing.

At one point in my life, I was really busy. I was working a nine-to-five job helping kids with disabilities gain inclusion into community programs. To make ends meet, I took a job for an hour or so before work three days a week. In addition, I taught a few night classes after work. I was sharing custody of two adorable young daughters, so I got to experience a bit of single parenting on the days I did not teach. On the weekends that my children shared with their mom, I commuted to grad school in San Francisco, which is about a five-hour drive from my house. To study well takes time. To teach well takes time. To perform well at a nine-to-five job also takes time. To keep up with a household takes time. I have to say however, that of all those activities, parenting was perhaps the most exhilarating and the most tiring. I do not claim that I did all those activities as well as someone else might have, but it was a busy time for me.

Teaching college freshmen and sophomores allows me a chance to observe lots of activity on campus. Students frequently let you know how busy their lives are (especially if their papers are due). From what I can observe, much of that activity requires that they stay connected to a large network of fellow students. They have calls to place, text messages to peck out, calls to answer, instant messages to instantly respond to, and even an occasional book to read, test to take, or assignment to finish. In short, they are very busy. My fellow instructors are also extremely busy. There are projects to grade, books to write, studies to publish, conferences to organize and attend, not to mention classes to teach.

There is, however, a rhythm to academia that is comforting to most of us. Fall brings new students to meet and, more importantly as far as some of us are concerned, football season. Eventually classes end in time for a good winter holiday. If all goes as predicted in the summer, a bowl game will keep us distracted through the whole holiday season. Spring brings another term but that, too, is over in time for a really good summer recess. Some of us are even lucky enough to teach in a subject that interests us even after two or three decades of study. Yes, the college is busy, but the busy is fun.

My field of psychology has a lot to offer, but sometimes we get things terribly wrong. Some scientists, when first confronted with the enigma of autism, wondered in print why the mothers were not holding the children more often. Surely moms must be causing something that results in their children not attending as much as they should to their social environment. It turns out that the moms were just doing what responsive parents do; that is, trying to nurture and provide for their unique children as best as they could. It turns out that their children were just different than most of us were taught to expect that children were.

Another classic example has to do with activity and the old concept of hyperactivity. When I entered the field, our diagnostic manuals told us that children whose activity levels were two standard deviations above the norm for their age, sex, and socio-economic status were to be placed in the category of "hyperactive." (Even then it was a specious claim, as studies have since pointed out that there were actually no real norms for activity, much less measures of distribution like standard deviations for that trait). It was, however, a diagnosis that made its way into the culture and gained a lot of popular support from harried teachers, stressed-out moms and dads, and those who like to pontificate about such things on television talk shows. The trouble is, it just didn't pan out. It turns out that the problem is that "over activity" is not the hallmark of children who are struggling in elementary school. The problem is the inability to attend for a reasonable amount of time to low levels of sensory stimulation (i.e., school). Once we realized that and changed the label to reflect the attention deficit, the treatments became more effective.

Children highlight for us another part of the problem of being busy. No one would argue that most children are pretty active. Scientists even remind us that many of the skills that they will need in adulthood are developed as they play. Another way to frame that is that their play is their work. As they get older, though, we introduce chores and other things that seem clearly outside of the realm of play, and struggles often ensue. It does not take a degree in behavioral science to make the work/play distinction with children. If left to their own choosing, children play. In fact, they can be so busy playing that they forget to eat, take a bathroom break, or even rest. At my stage of life, it is hard to imagine something so fun that I could forget to do any of those three things for long.

As adults we face enormous pressure to stay busy. Men are still viewed as success objects by many in our culture. Going to work is a regular part of most of our days (not to imply that being at work and working are synonymous). In much the same way as women are judged by some based upon their looks or their sex appeal (sex objects is the common term), men are often evaluated based upon their position in relation to the vocational realm (success objects). Women may also bear the double burden of being expected to be busy with both career and family, clearly a higher work load than was ever healthy. Even when we are officially on vacation, there is a tremendous amount to be done. (Most larger families like my own cannot travel anywhere for long without a lot of preparation and planning.) Much of the satisfaction that couples feel or do not feel in their relationship has to do with how each individual feels about the other person's level of work output. It may be a simple negotiation over who takes out the garbage or a complex, never-ending discussion over the care and feeding of the children. Either way, this perception of the shared nature of the workload is a powerful force in keeping people happy or keeping them in a chronic state of unhappiness. Professional marriage counselors call that phenomenon "perceived reciprocity."

The result of this struggle, and a myriad of other cultural forces, is that the desire to at least appear busy permeates much of modern life. If you follow the verbal behavior as I do, you will also notice that there is not even a clear correlation between how busy folks are and how much of their time is spent describing how busy they are. It makes sense really. If you are thought of as busy already, there might be disinclination to give you more work to do. Conversely, if you are seen as not busy, someone might just give you some of their work to do.

In my house it goes something like this. It starts with a casual-sounding inquiry along the lines of "Hey, what are you doing?" I have found that these inquiries are not always simple curiosity about what I am actually doing. Instead they are often an attempt to see if the activity that currently occupies my time is the type that can be suspended or interrupted for sufficient time to allow me to participate in the activity that is currently occupying the other person's time (folding something, moving something, lifting something, going somewhere else, buying something, or whatever it may be). Over the years I have grown more aware of this delicate negotiation.

The simple fact is that despite a fairly normal level of activity, there are indeed times that most would not think of as me being busy. I might be prone on a couch with my eyes closed (clearly pondering the latest child development research). I might be putting a little white ball into a cup (clearly establishing my "pre-exercise" routine). Or I could even be engrossed in watching a college football game on TV. It may not sound just right, but to those who know me well, I am clearly "busy watching football."

978-0-595-38120-3
0-595-38120-0